TRACING YOUR FAMILY'S GENEALOGICAL HISTORY BY RECORDS

STEP BY STEP INSTRUCTIONAL GUIDE TO TRACE YOUR FAMILY'S NATIVE TRIBE

Providing information is not the same as providing advice. Therefore, the information provided within this publication is provided for educational purposes only, and with the understanding that the various authors, editors and/or publishers are not engaged in rendering any advice. As such, the information provided within this publication should not be used as a substitute for consulting professionals such as genealogists or competent entities alike.

While we have made every attempt to ensure that the information contained within this publication is accurate and from what we believe to be reliable sources, we are not responsible for any errors or omissions, or for the results obtained from the use of the information. Use of the information contained herein is at the user's own risk.

While every effort has been made to ensure the reliability of the information presented in the publication, Im Just Here To Make You Think Inc. (IJHTMYT), nor the author of this publication, does not guarantee the accuracy of the data contained herein. IJHTMYT, nor the author of this publication accepts no payment for listing; and inclusion in the publication of any organizations, agency, institution, publication, service, or individual does not imply endorsement of the editors or publisher. Errors brought to the attention of the publisher and verified to the satisfaction of the publisher will be corrected in future editions.

This publication is a creative work fully protected by all applicable copyright laws, as well as by misappropriation, trade secret, unfair competition, and other applicable laws. The authors and editors of this work have added value to the underlying factual material herein through one or more of the following: unique and original selection, coordination, expression, arrangement, and classification of the information. All rights to this publication will be vigorously defended.

Copyright © 2016
Im Just Here To Make You Think Inc.
All rights reserved.

ISBN-13: 978-1729514511
ISBN-10: 1729514510

TRACING YOUR FAMILY'S GENEALOGICAL HISTORY BY RECORDS

Dane Calloway

CONTENTS

1. Find Out What Your Relatives Already Know   1
2. Beginning Your Genealogy Research   7
3. Adopted Children   13
4. Tracing Your Family's Associated Tribe   17
5. National Archives   23
6. Personal Computer Use   27
7. Freedman's Bank Accounts   31
8. Dawes Rolls   39
9. Wallace Rolls And Guion Miller Rolls   43
10. Indian Census Rolls   51
11. Microfilm Publications For Genealogical And Historical Research   57

FIND OUT WHAT YOUR RELATIVES ALREADY KNOW
(CHAPTER 1)

While assisting people with this step, I noticed the similarities in which each family would tend to have useful information concerning their family's background already in their possession, but it falls short due to some families underestimating the power of this information.

Well, wouldn't you be happy to know that I was once in that same predicament?

For starters, it is very likely that one of your many relatives began to compile a family tree a long time ago.

Researching family history was a very difficult task before the days of the Internet arose, so they might have gave up their search but also stored that useful information nearby.

An older version of the family tree could very well incorporate information from relatives who are no longer alive.

But even if you are the first, you should still be able to collect a lot of information by asking your relatives the right questions.

Just do not expect them to have the perfect memories of course, or to remember everything on the spur of the moment.

In fact, you will often find that if you go back to someone with bits of information you have gleaned from other relatives, or perhaps an old photo you've found, it helps to unlock other memories. It is amazing how the little things can bring it all back for most people.

So when you talk to your relatives, be sure to begin with simple questions like "How many brothers and sisters did your father/mother have?" for example, then maybe follow up with "Who was the oldest/youngest" and so on.

Have fun. Smile with rejoice in your research. Become an investigative reporter and really just have an open conversation with your relatives.

Now mind you, do not expect people to remember exact dates of birth (though in most cases they will), but a birthday or an approximate age will be a great deal of help in your research for records later on.

At this particular stage, it is also very important and highly useful to gather information about where your ancestors originated from specifically, and maybe even direct locations of birth if someone knows exactly.

Find out all of what your relatives know, even if some information might be inaccurate, because sometimes elder relatives can forget things about their origins, and that's perfectly fine because they gave you a grounding to work with.

Record the information you gather either by writing it down or, what I like to do is, video record it with maybe a video camera or a camera phone. Store this information safely because you will be returning to it later on as a reference.

BEGINNING YOUR GENEALOGY RESEARCH
(CHAPTER 2)

Begin your research in the most current records rather than the older more historic records. In other words, research from present to past and not past to present to make things a lot easier on yourself.

What is also important to note, do not begin your genealogical research on your family within Indian records, on and offline, for this can most often lead you towards a dead-end without the necessary information available yet to bring about the proper most accurate results. You will get to this step later on.

Your research should begin in non-Indian records for right now, or rather other public records, such as records maintained by State, local and federal governments, churches, schools and/or the Freedman's Bank, unless a relative is currently a member of a federally recognized tribe.

You should find all the information you can about your parents, grandparents, and more distant ancestors and write such information down or video record it as I mentioned earlier.

The most important information is vital statistics, including ancestral names (if applicable), dates of birth, marriages (or divorces) deaths, and also the places where your ancestors were born, lived, married, and died, i.e. birth certificates (very important), death records (very important), marriage certificates, etc.

You may contact your local vital statistics building in your State to request that you receive the original copy of these records mentioned above.

Note that some States may charge a small fee for the records, and some States require that immediate children of either the mother or father (or grandparents or great grandparents) are the only people that could have access to those records. I highly recommend that you call their office before going there to be sure first.

In a few States, I noticed that the department will allow you to print off the records online, but note that this copy you print is not a physical copy nor an official birth/death record copy, it is a receipt that can not be used officially when filing for tribal membership purposes for example.

You may also contact any National Archives of the United States throughout the country, and order an official copy of your relative's records. A fee may be required in this case as well.

Be advised that you are looking to see which biological parent, grandparent and/or great grandparent has either "Negro", "Colored" or "Col." as their classification of race on the records that you have gathered, but more importantly on their birth certificates.

If in fact your grandparents and/or great grandparents' records (specifically their birth certificates) indicates those classifications of race as I just mentioned, then they are in fact Natives of America. Hold on to those records, you would need to reference them later on.

ADOPTED CHILDREN
(CHAPTER 3)

State agencies usually handles all adoptions in the United States. When a child is adopted, it typically happens in one of two ways that is very important to note:

Families apply directly to adopt a child through foster care, or first become foster parents and then adopt after the biological parents' rights are terminated by the State in a court setting.

I briefly mentioned both ways due to each case being slightly different when it comes to accurately researching the proper records necessary to begin the process.

Those of you who are in fact adopted and are seeking to research your genealogy must have access to the following:

1. Your Adoption Records
2. Court Ordered Adoption Certificates
3. Biological Mother and/or Father's Names
4. Name of Foster Care or Foster Parents

With these documents handy, you may either call the Foster Care organization that processed the adoption, or the courts that handled the case in order to grant the adoption.

Depending on which one is applicable to your case. Note that you are looking to retrieve the information you need, about your biological parents, to proceed with Step 2 as mentioned earlier.

Mind you, this is your legal right to have this information, but I am sure different States has different rules, policies and procedures, but it shouldn't halt you from gaining access to the information you need.

I highly recommend speaking with a case manager if it's a Foster Care, or if you must deal with the courts, speaking with a court's clerk should be of great assistance as well.

Be sure to gather all information possible that is available. Especially your relative's dates of birth, direct locations of birth (and death if applicable).

Official copies of these records are a must in order to proceed with Step 2. If you are having trouble with retrieving this information, do not hesitate to call my office line located on the website for further assistance and additional information.

TRACING YOUR FAMILY'S ASSOCIATED TRIBE
(CHAPTER 4)

Once you have gathered all of the necessary records as I mentioned in Step 1 and Step 2, then and only then are you able to continue with this step.

There are currently multiple different ways to trace your family's association to a native tribe. One quick easier method is by location of birth.

With your great grandparents original location and year of birth handy, you should be able to determine which tribe/nation they were associated with by viewing official tribal maps (Atlas) of the many American Indian territories, villages and reservations.

To attach some useful references to the equation, you can follow the links that I have provided below for further information and assistance with tribal locations in the United States, Alaska, Canada and Mexico:

- **American Indians and Alaska Natives in the United States Wall Map**[1] - Map of American Indian geographic areas by name of the village or reservation. Viewable or downloadable in .gif or .pdf formats. *Source: U.S. Census Bureau, Geography Division, Cartographic Operations Branch, 2002*

---

[1] Link: https://www2.census.gov/geo/maps/special/aian_wall/aian_wall_map.htm

- **American Indians and Alaska Natives in the United States Wall Map**[2] - Provides 2000 - 2011 versions of maps of American Indian geographic areas by name of the village or reservation. Viewable or downloadable in .gif or .pdf formats. *Source: U.S. Census Bureau, Geography Division, Cartographic Operations Branch, 2000 - 2011*

- **2010 Census: Tribal Tract Reference Maps**[3] - These federal American Indian reservation-based maps show and label tribal census tracts and tribal block groups as delineated to support 2010 Census data dissemination. These maps also show the boundaries and names of American Indian reservations, off-reservation trust lands (ORTLs), Alaska Native areas, Hawaiian home lands, states, counties, county subdivisions, and places. Additionally, these maps display a base feature network including roads, railroads, and water bodies. These features are labeled as map scale permits.

Each entity is covered by one or more parentmap sheets at a single scale. An index map showing the sheet configuration is included for all entities requiring more than one parent map sheet. *Source: U.S. Census Bureau, Geography Division, Carto- graphic Operations Branch, 2010*

---

[2] Source: https://www.census.gov/geo/maps-data/maps/aian_wall_maps.html
[3] Source: https://www.census.gov/geo/maps-data/maps/2010tribaltract.html

- **U.S. Federal and State Indian Reservations Map**[4] - Not quite as detailed but it does include links to American Indian place names, glossary and American Indians by the Numbers (compilations from the Census). *Source: Infoplease, 2000 - 2017*

- **1911 Indians in the United States Map**[5] - This Historical Map of Indians of the United States illustrates the Indian portages, the Cessions of Indian lands, 1816 - 1830; and removal of the Southern Indians, 1830 - 1834. The map also depicts the National Indian Reservations in 1905, and shows approximate locations of the Indian tribes (thus: Dakotas) at the time of their chief historical importance. The Californian, and other tribes along the Pacific coast, were allegedly too numerous to be indicated in any details. *Source: University of Texas at Austin - Historical Atlas by William Shepherd, 1911*

- **Tribal Nations Map**[6] - Map of Canada and the Continental U.S. showing the original locations and names of Native American tribes, even the names of tribes that were forgotten. *Source: Aaron Carapella, 2014*

- **Indigenous Nations of Mexico**[7] - This particular map of Mexico features both the original and commonly known names of some Indigenous Nations. *Source: Aaron Carapella, 2014*

---

[4] Source: https://www.infoplease.com/us/race-population/us-federal-and-state-indian-reservations
[5] Source: http://www.emersonkent.com/map_archive/native_american_1911.htm
[6] Source: http://www.npr.org/assets/news/2014/06/Tribal_Nations_Map_NA.pdf
[7] Source: http://www.npr.org/assets/news/2014/06/Tribal_Map_Mexico.pdf

NATIONAL ARCHIVES
(CHAPTER 5)

You may also find lots of very useful data relating to your family by searching through the billions of historical records housed inside a National Archives facility.

With your previous documents/records and information handy, you may search for things like historical Census records[8], Military service records (specifically the War of 1812, Civil War, WWI and WWII), Naturalization records, Immigration Records, Vital records, Court records, etc. all located at their facility.

Now, if you are unable to travel to a facility, you may also order copies of specific records you discover online (as mentioned in Step 6) as you please via their official website[9].

However, ordering records from the National Archives website may have a cost if you prefer to do things online, otherwise, walking into a facility is a different story all together.

In all actuality, I highly recommend that you do make the trip to any National Archives facility if you can. This will immediately grant you free access to a much broader variety of hands-on data to research from.

---

[8] Source: https://www.archives.gov/research/census
[9] Source: https://eservices.archives.gov/orderonline/start.swe?SWECmd=Start&SWEHo=eservices.archives.gov

You are also granted free access to these enormous database sites (listed below), from a link on Archives.gov while literally at any National Archives facility itself, or at almost all Libraries across the United States.

These links will expand the utilitarian data that you will have access to, without having a subscription, only if these links are accessed directly at a National Archives branch or at a public Library:

- **Ancestry**[10]
- **Fold3**[11]

---

[10] Source: https://www.ancestry.com/wiz/?s_kwcid=ancestry&gclid=EAIaIQobChMIpcur2_i61gIVj4WzCh06kA6yEAAYASADEgLJ3PD_BwE&o_xid=21837&o_lid=21837&o_sch=Paid+Search+Non+Brand

[11] Source: http://www.fold3.com/institution-index.php

PERSONAL COMPUTER USE
(CHAPTER 6)

This method is only recommend for those that absolutely can not make it to a National Archives facility or a public Library. There is in fact a great deal of information online that can be accessed for FREE, and without a subscription of some sort. These sites are:

- **Archives Catalog Advanced Search**[12] - Provides the free data available online from what you type in the searches bar. This is a very informative and useful tool. I personally collected data of my relatives using this method. Note: Some data may not being viewable due to some records having a small cost. Also, try not to be vague when entering information for a search, if you do so, your results will vary.

- **Family Search**[13] - Provides free access to a database of records from around the world, including many provided from the National Archives.

- **Castle Garden**[14] - Provides free access to a database containing entries for 10 million immigrants from 1830 through 1892. Search- able by passenger name, the database provides information including age, sex, literacy, occupation, country of origin, port of embarkation, date of arrival into New York, and ship name.

---

[12] Source: https://catalog.archives.gov/advancedsearch
[13] Source: http://www.familysearch.org/
[14] Source: http://www.castlegarden.org/

FREEDMAN'S BANK ACCOUNTS
(CHAPTER 7)

There is also a hidden gem, in my opinion, located inside of the National Archives that many people maybe very unfamiliar with..

The intel surrounding the Freedman's Bank is very essential to one's research and could possibly provide much more critical details about your family's genealogy.

Going back to the year of 1861, Colored and White Northern Abolitionists pushed for the creation of a Freedman's Bank.

These banks were said to have helped former slaves with developing positive habits of financial responsibility, while allegedly assisting their transition from slavery to freedom.

So four years later, on the date of March 3rd, 1865, Congress created The Freedmen's Savings and Trust Company, which was later referred to as The Freedman's Bank.

According to historical Congressional records, President Lincoln immediately signed the bill into law. Deposits were received only "by or on behalf of persons heretofore held in slavery in the United States, or their descendants."

Up to 7% interest was allowed for deposits, and any unclaimed accounts were to be pooled into a charitable fund that was used to educate the children of former slaves.

In 1868 the bank headquarters was moved to Washington, District of Columbia (D.C.), where "Colored" staffers were trained to take over its operations.

At its peak, the bank operated 37 branches in seventeen different states and the District of Columbia, making it one of the first multi-state banks in the nation. And by 1870, nearly all of the local branches were operated by people of color, or rather Copper-Colored Indigenous Aborigines.

Frederick Douglass, who was elected president in 1874, donated tens of thousands of dollars of his own funds to the institution, but due to some alleged fraudulent activity amongst the bank's upper management and board of directors, the bank was forced to close officially on June 29th 1874.

In my opinion, I feel as though that was a malicious manipulated story designed to have reason to close all 37 branches of the Freedman's banks. I wouldn't put it past a jealous government of a corporation anyway.

Furthermore, at the date of closing, get this - nearly $3 million dollars was owed to 61,144 depositors (possibly your relatives). Now adjusting these numbers for inflation, that's nearly $57.8 million dollars and over 70 thousand depositors.

I stated all of this to inform you that the records of those accounts are located in the National Archives facilities still till this very day, and those records also included very useful information like one's first name and last name given, their date of birth, their location of birth, their current residence of that time period, their alleged classification of race, and many other useful historic resources that is not commonly known to the public. I will list what is available online for free:

- **National Archives Microfilm Publication M816 Registers of Signatures of Depositors in Branches of the Freedman's Savings and Trust Company, 1865 - 1874**[15] - This collection consists of an index and images of registers for 67,000 people who opened accounts in the Freedman's Savings and Trust Company. The records are from Record Group 101 Records of the Office of the Comptroller of the Currency. The registers identify those who opened accounts. Because the Freedman's Bank was required by law to protect the interests of depositors' heirs, the branches collected an enormous amount of personal information about each depositor and his or her family when the account was opened. The registers cover

---

[15] Source: https://www.familysearch.org/wiki/en/United_States,_Freedman%27s_Bank_Records_(FamilySearch_Historical_Records)

approximately the years 1865 to 1874. Each register book consists of printed forms, with information for four depositors on each page. The registers are arranged chronologically by the date the account was established and then numerically by account number. Many numbers are missing, a few are out of order, and some blocks of numbers were never used. Many registers seem to be missing.

- **National Archives Microfilm Publication M817, Indexes to Deposit Ledgers in Branches of the Freedman's Savings and Trust Company, 1865 - 1874**[16] - This database is an index to Freedman's Savings and Trust Company's registers of signatures of depositors. Some information that may be found in this index includes: Name of depositor, Date of application/deposit, Name of employer, Name of plantation, Age, Height, Complexion, Name of father and/or mother, Whether married, Place of birth, Residence, Occupation, Names of children, Names of brothers and sisters. Note: Not all entries will contain all of this information, and this database may need to be accessed at a National Archives branch or a Public Library to be utilized for free, unless you have a subscription by now.

---

[16] Source: http://search.ancestry.com/search/db.aspx?dbid=8755

- **Records of Post-Civil War Federal Agencies at the National Archives, Reference Information Paper 108, 2010**[17]

Do I believe that this money is owed to the descendants of these specific depositors?

Yes, but not enough people are cognizant of this information currently, so attempting to go after it would take a group effort, in my opinion, once all records have been retrieved first. By doing so, that will prevent the Federal Government from removing the actual proof that is currently available at this time.

---

[17] Source: https://www.google.com/url?sa=t&source=web&rct=j&url=https://www.archives.gov/files/publications/ref-info-papers/rip108.pdf&ved=0ahUKEwiv59etz7rWAhVMKiYKHYRzBwgQFggyMAI&usg=AFQjCNGj06yMWz-x7PqZpYXqT1eP4NFBLA

DAWES ROLLS
(CHAPTER 8)

The Dawes Commission, known formally as the Commission to the Five Civilized Tribes, was appointed by President Grover Cleveland in 1893 and headed by Henry L. Dawes to negotiate land with the Cherokee, Creek, Choctaw, Chickasaw and Seminole tribes.

The tribe members were allotted land in return for abolishing tribal governments and recognizing Federal laws. In order to receive the land (or a share of common property), individual tribal members first had to apply and be deemed eligible by the Commission.

Heads of families, orphans, and children would receive from 40 up to 160 acres of land by proving their tribal membership.

The Commission accepted applications from 1898 until 1907, with a few additional people accepted by an Act of Congress in 1914. The resulting lists of those who were accepted as eligible for land became known as the Dawes Rolls:

• **Applications for Enrollment with the Five Civilized Tribes**[18] - These records have also been referred to as the "Dawes Enrollment Applications" or the "Dawes Enrollment Jackets." These records are arranged by tribe, thereunder by enrollment category (By Blood, Doubtful, or Rejected), and thereunder numerically by

---
[18] Source: https://catalog.archives.gov/id/617283

enrollment ("census") card number. This link provides records containing over 101,000 names currently, and can be searched to discover the enrollee's name, sex, blood degree, and census card number. Census cards often provide additional genealogical information and can contain references to earlier rolls, such as the 1880 Cherokee census. A census card is often accompanied by an "application jacket." The jackets can contain valuable supporting documentation such as birth and death affidavits, marriage licenses, and correspondence.

- **Allotment Files for the Five Civilized Tribes**[19] - This link provides you free access to the many utilitarian allotment records held by FamilySearch.

Today these five tribes continue to use the Dawes Rolls as the basis for determining their individual tribal membership. They usually require applicants to provide proof of descent from a person who is listed on these rolls. If you found your ancestor(s) on the Dawes Roll, then you may contact the tribes directly for enrollment information by following the links provided below:

- **Cherokee Nation**[20]
- **Choctaw Nation**[21]
- **Creek Nation**[22]
- **Seminole Nation**[23]
- **Chickasaw Nation**[24]

---

[19] Source: https://familysearch.org/search/collection/1390101
[20] Source: http://www.cherokee.org/Home/section/services/service/Registration
[21] Source: https://www.choctawnation.com/
[22] Source: http://www.muscogeenation-nsn.gov/
[23] Source: http://sno-nsn.gov/
[24] Source: http://www.chickasaw.net/

WALLACE ROLLS AND GUION MILLER ROLLS
(CHAPTER 9)

The Wallace Rolls were created because the Cherokee citizenship of many ex-slaves of the Cherokee in Indian Territory was disputed by the Cherokee tribe.

The establishment of their status was important in determining their right to live on Cherokee land and to share in certain annuity and other payment, including a special $75,000 award voted by Congress on October 19, 1888.

A series of investigations was conducted in order to compile the rolls of the Cherokee Freedmen.

John W. Wallace compiled the original rolls for the Authenticated, Admitted, and Rejected Freedmen, and the Free Negroes.

Because of discrepancies, additional supplements were added. Individual entries give name, age, sex, residence, and other pertinent information.

The individual rolls are generally arranged alphabetically by initial letter of surname of head of family, but occasionally they may first be divided into groups and districts. You may search the Wallace Rolls here:

- **Revised Copies Of The Wallace Rolls**[25] - This link provides the Index to the Revised Copies of Cherokee Citizenship Rolls Called the "Wallace Rolls," 1890 - 1896

UPDATE: On August 30th 2017, a US District Judge named Thomas Hogan ruled that Cherokee Freedmen (and their descendants) can now officially join the Cherokee Nation, the second-largest tribe in the United States. I have since provided more information here[26] detailing the results. According to the National Archives, the U.S. Court of Claims ruled in favor of the Eastern Cherokee Tribe's claim against the U.S. on May 18, 1905. This resulted in the appropriation of $1 million to the Tribe's eligible individuals and families.

Interior Department employee Guion Miller created a list using several rolls and applications to verify tribal enrollment for the distribution of funds.

The applications received documented over 125,000 individuals; the court approved more than 30,000 individuals to share in the funds. To be approved for funds the individual must:

- Be alive as of May 28, 1906

- Establish that he/she was a member or descendants of a person that had been included in the forced removal to Indian Territory, known as the "Ross Party"

---
[25] Source: https://catalog.archives.gov/id/300344
[26] Source: http://wp.me/p7Q8Fh-I1

• Not be affiliated with a tribe other than the Cherokee

• Submit an application that had to be received by August 31, 1907. Parents or guardians were given the opportunity to apply for minors and persons of unsound mind. Most of these later applications were rejected due to late receipt; however, all contain important individual and family history information.

These applications includes:

• Applicant's English and Indian names, date and place of birth

• Names and ages of brothers and sisters

• Place of birth and date of death of parents and grandparents

• Residence

• Spouse and children

• Names of extended family

In certifying the eligibility of the Cherokees, Guion Miller used earlier census lists and rolls that had been made of the Cherokees by Hester, Chapman, Drennen, and others between 1835 and 1884.

Copies of some of these rolls and the indexes to them are filed with the Guion Miller records and are filmed as part of the publications only made available on Fold3.com (databased titled "Guion Miller Roll") and Ancestry.com (databased titled "U.S., Records Related to Enrollment of Eastern Cherokee by Guion Miller, 1908-1910") if you choose to search online and do not mind paying for it of course, otherwise, you may walk inside any National Archives branch and utilize their computers for free access to these records.

What is very important to note, other enrollment records used by Gu- ion Miller are among the "classified fields" of the Bureau, and are designed as "33931-11-053 Cherokee Nation."

You may search through the Guion Miller Rolls Index online for free to see if any relatives of yours has submitted an application for the Guion Miller Roll below:

• **Applications Submitted for the Eastern Cherokee Roll of 1909**[27] - This index includes some names of persons applying for compensation arising from the judgment of

---

[27] Source: https://catalog.archives.gov/id/300330

the United States Court of Claims on May 28, 1906, for the Eastern Cherokee tribe. While numerous individuals applied, not all the claims were allowed. The information included on the index is the application number, the name of the applicant, and the State or Territory in which the individual resided at the time the application was filed.

To order copies of these records of the original applications, you must submit a completed NATF Form 83 which includes the individual's name and application number. A separate form must be completed for each file you wish copied.

To obtain an NATF Forms 83 write the National Archives, NWCTB, Old Military and Civil Records (Form 83), Washington, D.C. 20408.

If you found your ancestor(s) on the Wallace Rolls and/or the Guion Miller Rolls, then you may contact the Cherokee Nation directly for enrollment information by following the link provided below:

- **Cherokee Nation**[28]

---

[28] Source: http://www.cherokee.org/Home/section/services/service/Registration

INDIAN CENSUS ROLLS
(CHAPTER 10)

The Indian Census Rolls were undertaken by the Bureau of Indian Affairs (BIA), from about 1885 to 1940.

These are the names of persons who were actually living amongst their tribes, under the supervision of a BIA agent on reservation lands.

These censuses were compiled and returned each year to the Commissioner of Indian Affairs, however, not all tribes are included and not all years are covered. Sometimes agents were unable to complete them for obvious reasons.

These Rolls were also microfilmed by the National Archives (link to download the pdf summary of M595[29]), and they have been digitized and made available on the Internet.

If you can make the trip to one of National Archives branches, then you can use their computers to undertake your research for free. Otherwise, you will be assessed a subscription fee for the sites I will list below. Mind you, you may find these links free of services at your local libraries as well:

• **Indian Census Rolls via Fold**[30] These are the censuses of all the tribes, except the Five Civilized Tribes in Oklahoma, from about 1885 to 1940. They do not include everyone who was an Indian, only those living on reservations.

---

[29] Source: https://www.google.com/url?sa=t&source=web&rct=j&url=https://www.archives.gov/files/research/microfilm/m595.pdf&ved
[30] Source: http://www.fold3.com/institution-index.php

Directions: Select "All Titles" and choose "Indian Census Rolls." You do have options of searching with a name or you can click on Browse, choose the tribe, and search individual rolls yourself. This will allow you to check out all the possibilities for names and see if any seem to be your relatives.

• **Indian Census Rolls via Ancestry**[31] - This link directs you to the lists everything Ancestry has in terms of Native American Records.

Directions: Once you are at the site, select "US Indian Census Rolls." You are able to select the "category" you want to research and you can type in your ancestor's name in the "search box" as well.

In Conclusion of this Section

After you have completed your genealogical research, documented your ancestry, and determined the tribe with which your ancestor was affiliated, you are ready to contact the tribe directly to obtain the criteria for membership.

Rarely is the BIA involved in enrollment and membership. Each tribe determines whether an individual is eligible for membership. Each tribe maintains its own enrollment records and records about past members. To obtain information about your eligibility for membership, you must contact the tribe.

---
[31] Source: http://search.ancestryinstitution.com/search/group/nativeamerican

The Tribal Leaders Directory[32] that is published by the Bureau of Indian Affairs lists all 562 federally recognized American Indian Tribes and Alaska Natives. It also lists all the Regions, Agencies and Offices within the BIA.

---

[32] Source: https://www.bia.gov/tribal-leaders-directory

MICROFILM PUBLICATIONS FOR GENEALOGICAL AND HISTORICAL RESEARCH
(CHAPTER 11)

This reference guide contains a list of various records useful for research that are available on microfilm at the National Archives at Fort Worth (2600 West 7th Street, 76107). Other microfilm publications are available for viewing on Ancestry.com or Fold3.com. While at the National Archives, it is currently free to search & print from both Ancestry & Fold3.

PASSENGER LISTS, INDEXES, & RELATED RECORDS

M2102 Letters Sent & Registers of Letters Received by the Secretary of the Treasury, 1882 1887 Relating to Immigration Matters.

T517 Carolina, 1890 - 1924 Index to Passenger Lists of Vessels Arriving at Ports in Alabama, Florida, Georgia, & South

A3435* Crew Lists of Vessels Arriving at (1947 1957) & Passenger Lists of Vessels Departing from (1946 - 1948) Alexandria, Virginia

M334 Supplemental Index to Passenger Lists of Vessels Arriving at Atlantic & Gulf Coast Ports (Excluding New York), 1820 1874

M326 Index to Passenger Lists of Vessels Arriving at Baltimore, Maryland, 1833 1866

M327 Index to Passenger Lists of Vessels Arriving at Baltimore, Maryland, 1820 1897

T520 Index (Soundex) to Passenger Lists of Vessels Arriving at Baltimore, Maryland, 1897 July 1952

T521 Index to Passenger Lists of Vessels Arriving at Boston, Massachusetts, 1902 1906

T617 Index to Passenger Lists of Vessels Arriving at Boston, Massachusetts, July 1, 1906 Dec. 31, 1920

A3423 Passenger & Crew Lists of Airplanes Arriving at Brownsville, Texas, Jan. 1943 - Sept. 1964

M1514* Indexes of Vessels Arriving at Brownsville, Texas, 19351955; Houston, Texas, 19481954; at Port Arthur & Beaumont, Texas, 1908 - 1954; & at Lake Charles, Louisiana, 1908 - 1954

M2040 Index to Manifests of Permanent & Statistical Arrivals at Eagle Pass, Texas, 1929 - 1953

A3465 Index to Transatlantic Vessel Arrivals & Departures from Eastern United States & Canadian Ports, 1904 1939

A3457 Crew Lists of Vessels Arriving at Eastport, Maine, 19491958

A3406 No statistical Manifests & Statistical Index Cards of Aliens Arriving at El Paso, Texas, 1905 - 1927

M2095 Lists of Passengers Arriving & Departing from the District of Fairfield, Connecticut

M1357 Index to Passenger Lists of Vessels Arriving at Galveston, Texas, 1896 - 1906

M1358 Index to Passenger Lists of Vessels Arriving at Galveston, Texas, 1906 - 1951

M1842 Passenger Lists of Vessels Arriving at Georgetown, South Carolina, 1923 - 1939, & at Apalachicola, Boynton, Boca Grande, Carrabelle, Fernandina, Fort Pierce, Hobe Sound, Lake Worth, Mayport, Millville, Port Ingush, Port St. Joe, St. Andrews, & Stuart, Florida, 1904-1942

T523* Index to Passengers Arriving at Gulfport, Florida, August 27, 1904 - August 28, 1954

M1778* Passenger & Crew Lists of Vessels Departing the Trust Territory of the Pacific Islands for Arrival at Guam, 1947 - 1952, & Related Records

A3448 Manifests of Alien Arrivals at Havre, Loring, Orpheum, Raymond, Turner, Westby, & White Tail, Montana, 1924 - 1956

A3437 Manifests of Statistical & Some No statistical Alien Arrivals at Laredo, Texas, May 1903 - April 1955

T522 Index to Passengers Arriving at New Bedford, Massachusetts, July 1, 1902 - November 18, 1954

T527 Index to Passenger Lists of Vessels Arriving at New Orleans, Louisiana, before 1900

T618 Index to Passenger Lists of Vessels Arriving at New Orleans, Louisiana, 1900 - 1952 7RA192 Crew Lists, New Orleans District, 1803 - 1825

M261 Index to Passenger Lists of Vessels Arriving at New York, New York, 1820 - 1846

M1066 Registers of Vessels Arriving at New York, New York, 1789 - 1919

A3464 Indexes to Vessels Arriving at New York, New York, 1897 - 1956

T621 Index (Soundex) to Passenger Lists of Vessels Arriving at New York, New York, July 1, 1902, December 31, 1943.

M1417 Index (Soundex) to Passengers Arriving in New York, New York, 1944 - 1948

M2027* Admitted Alien Crew Lists of Vessels Arriving at Pascagoula, Mississippi, July 1903, May 1935

M360 Index to Passenger Lists of Vessels Arriving at Philadelphia, Pennsylvania, 1800 - 1906

T526 Index (Soundex) Cards, Ship Arrivals at Philadelphia, Pennsylvania, Jan. 1, 1883 - June 28, 1948

T791 Book Indexes, Philadelphia, Pennsylvania, Lists, 1906 - 1926

A3441 Manifests of Alien Arrivals at Port Huron, Michigan, February 1902 - December 1952

T793 Book Indexes, Portland, Maine, Passenger Lists, 1907 - 1930

A3466 Manifests of Alien Arrivals at Presidio, Texas, ca. 1911 - 1955

T792 Book Indexes, Providence, Rhode Island, Passenger Lists, 1911 - 1934

T518 Index to Passengers Arriving at Providence, Rhode Island, June 18, 1911 - Oct. 5 1954

A3456 Crew Lists of Vessels Arriving at Rochester, New York, 1944 - 1958

M1761 Index to Passenger Arrivals at San Diego, California, ca. 1904 ca. 1952

A3470* Chinese Passenger & Crew Lists of Vessels Arriving at San Diego, California, October 1905 - July 1923

M1437* Indexes to Vessels Arriving at San Francisco, 1882 - 1957

M1413 Registers of Chinese Laborers Returning to the U.S. through the Port of San Francisco, 1882 - 1888

A3480 Alien Certificates Issued to Aliens Pre-examined at Winnipeg, Manitoba, 1922 - 1929, Prior to Admission at the United States/Canada Border

RECORDS RELATING TO OWNERS & MASTERS OF SHIPS

M1857 Certificates of Enrollment Issued for Merchant Vessels at Galveston, Texas, 1846 - 1960 & 1865 - 1970, & Master Abstracts of Enrollments Issued for Merchant Vessels at All Texas Ports, 1846 - 1860 and 1865 - June 1911

M1863 Master Abstracts of Registers & Enrollments Issued for Merchant Vessels at North Carolina Ports, January 1815 - June 1911

M1862 Certificates of Enrollment Issued for Merchant Vessels at Cleveland, Ohio, April 1829 - May 1915

M1864 Certificates of Enrollment Issued for Merchant Vessels at Oswego, New York, 1815 - 1911

M2100 Certificates of Enrollment Issued for Merchant Vessels at Green Bay, Manitowoc, & Milwaukee, Wisconsin, 1851 - 1868

M2106 Master Abstracts of Certificates of Enrollments Issued for Merchant Vessels at Saint Louis, Missouri, 1846 - 1870

GENERAL RECORDS RELATING TO MILITARY SERVICE

M694 Index to Compiled Service Records of Volunteer Soldiers Who Served from 1784 - 1811

M2078* General Register of the United States Navy & Marine Corps, 1782 - 1882

T1102 Index to Navy Officers' Jackets, ("Officers Directory"), 1913 - 1925

M1785 Index to Pension Application Files of Remarried Widows after the Civil War

T316 Old War Index to Pension Files, 1815 - 1926 T318 Index to Indian Wars Pension Files, 1892 - 1926

A3442 Vessel & Organization Indexes to U.S. Navy Muster Rolls, 1892 - 1938 Revolutionary War Indexes

M860 General Index to compiled military service records of Revolutionary War Soldiers

M879* Index to compiled service records of American Naval Personnel who served during the Revolutionary War

M1051* Index to compiled service records of Revolutionary War Soldiers who served with the American Army in Georgia Military Organizations Revolutionary War Other Records

M1786* Record of Invalid Pension Payments to Veterans of the Revolutionary War, March 1801 - Sept. 1815

T1008* Register of Army Land Warrants Issued Under the Act of 1788, for Service in the Revolutionary War: Military District of Ohio.

War of 1812 Indexes

M229 Index to Compiled Service Records of Volunteer Soldiers Who Served During the War of 1812 in Organizations from the State of Louisiana

M250 Index to Compiled Service Records of Volunteer Soldiers Who Served during the War of 1812 in Organizations from the State of North Carolina

War of 1812 Compiled Service Records

M1829* Compiled Service Records of Major Uriah Blue's Detachment of Chickasaw Indians in the War of 1812

Creek War, 1836 - 1837

M244 Index to Compiled Service Records of Volunteer Soldiers Who Served During the Creek War in Organizations from the State of Alabama

Florida War, 1835 - 1842

M245* Index to Compiled Service Records of Volunteer Soldiers Who Served During the Florida War in Organizations from the State of Alabama

M239* Index to Compiled Service Records of Volunteer Soldiers Who Served During the Florida War in Organizations from the State of Louisiana

M241* Index to Compiled Service Records of Volunteer Soldiers Who Served During the War of 1837 - 1838 in Organizations from the State of Louisiana (Second Florida Campaign)

Patriot War, 1838 - 1839

M630* Index to Compiled Service Records of Volunteer Soldiers Who Served from the State of Michigan during the Patriot War

M631* Index to Compiled Service Records of Volunteer Soldiers Who Served from the State of New York During the Patriot War New York

Mexican War Indexes

T317 Index to Mexican War Pension Files, 1887 - 1926 Mexican War Compiled Service Records

M1970 Compiled service records of Volunteer soldiers who served during the Mexican War in Organizations from the state of Arkansas.

Civil War, Union

M532* Arizona Territory

M383 Arkansas

M536 Dakota

M537 Delaware

M538 District of Columbia

M264* Florida

M385 Georgia

M386 Kentucky

M387 Louisiana

M388 Maryland

M389* Mississippi

M547 Nebraska

M548 * Nevada

M242 New Mexico

M391 North Carolina

M552 Ohio

M553* Oregon

M392 Tennessee

M393 Texas

M556* Utah Territory

M394* Virginia

M558 Washington

M507 West Virginia

M589 Index to Compiled Service Records of Volunteer Union Soldiers Who Served with U.S. Colored Troops.

Civil War, Union Other Records

M823 Official Battle List of the Civil War, 1861 - 1865: Battle lists indicate which Union troops were engaged in particular Civil War operations. The battle lists in this publication are incomplete & reflect the numerous inaccuracies found in the original & secondary sources from which they were compiled. Still, they can serve as valuable tools in seeking out sources of data in Civil War related records.

M1523 Proceedings of U.S. Army Court-martials & Military Commissions of Union Soldiers Executed by U.S. Military Authorities, 1861 - 1866

Civil War, Confederate

M375* Arizona Territory

M376 Arkansas

M225 Florida

M226 Georgia

M377 Kentucky

M378 Louisiana

M379 Maryland

M232 Mississippi

M380 Missouri

M230 North Carolina

M381 South Carolina

M231 Tennessee

M227 Texas

M382 Virginia

M818 Index to Compiled Service Records of Confederate Soldiers Who Served in Organizations Raised Directly by the Confederate Government and of Confederate General and Staff Officers and Non-Regimental Enlisted Men.

Civil War, Confederate Compiled Service Records

M260 Records Relating to Confederate Naval & Marine Personnel

M836 Confederate States Army Casualties: Lists & Narrative Reports. The War with Spain

M240* Index to Compiled Service Records of Volunteer Soldiers Who Served During the War with Spain in Organizations from the State of Louisiana

M413 Index to Compiled Service Records of Volunteer Soldiers Who Served During the War with Spain in Organizations from the State of North Carolina

World War I

M1872* List of Mothers & Widows of American World War I Soldiers, Sailors, & Marines Entitled to Make a Pilgrimage to the War Cemeteries in Europe, 1930.

M2130 Stars & Stripes: Newspaper of the American Expeditionary Forces, 1981 - 1919. 90th Anniversary of the final issue of the World War I Stars & Stripes

World War II

M1730* Miscellaneous Documents Relating to the Japanese Attack on Pearl Harbor & Other Japanese Military Activities, 1941 - 1945.

M1738 Miscellaneous Documents Relating to the Atomic Bombing of Japan, Allied & Japanese Operations in the Pacific, & Japanese Reports on the Chinese Communist Party

Miscellaneous Military Records

M1856 Discharge certificates & miscellaneous records relating to the discharge of soldiers from the Regular Army, 1792 - 1815

M87 Records of the Commissioner of Claims (Southern Claims Commission), 1871 - 1880: Records of the commissioners appointed to receive & consider claims of citizens living in the Confederate states who had remained loyal to the government of the U.S. and whose property or supplies were taken for the use of the U.S. Army.

P2257 Summary Reports of Disallowed Claims (Southern Claims Commission), 1872 - 1875.

M91 Records Relating to the U.S. Military Academy, 1812 - 1867; records include nominations, resignations, & dismissal of cadets; appointment of instructors; courses of study; erection of buildings, etc.

M661 Historical Information Relating to Military Posts & Other Installations, ca. 1700 - 1900. Entries for permanent & temporary U.S. army posts; Confederate forts; fortified Indian towns; harbor pilot stations; national cemeteries; redoubt & batteries; civilian & fur company blockhouses; British, French, Spanish, & Dutch installations erected within the present boundaries of the United States.

M1635 Letters Received by the Headquarters of the Army, 1827 - 1903, (few rolls)

M858 Negroes in the Military Service of the United States, 1639 – 1886: A seven volume compilation of copies of official records, state papers, & historical extracts relating to the military status & service of blacks from the colonial period through 1886 prepared by the Colored Troops Division of the Adjutant General's Office, 1888

M929 Documents Relating to the Military & Naval Services of Blacks Awarded the Congressional Medal of Honor from Civil War to Spanish American War.

M2031* Selected Military Service Records Relating to Edgar Allen Poe

M2035* Selected Military Service & Pension Records Relating to Ulysses S. Grant

M2063* Selected Military Service Records Relating to Robert E. Lee

T251 List of Photographs & Photographic Negatives Relating to the War for the Union (War Department Subject Catalogue, No. 5, 1897)

M592 Proceedings of a Court Inquiry Concerning the Conduct of Major Marcus A. Reno at the Battle of the Little Big Horn River on June 25 and 26, 1876

T1027* Records Relating to the Army Career of Henry O. Flipper, 1873 - 1882

BUREAU OF REFUGEES, FREEDMEN, & ABANDONED LANDS

M742 Selected Series of Records Issued by Commissioner for the Bureau of Refugees, Freedmen, & Abandoned Lands, 1865 - 1872

M752 Registers & Letters Received by the Commissioner for the Bureau of Refugees, Freedmen, & Abandoned Lands, 1865 - 1872

M809 Records of the Assistant Commissioner for the State of Alabama, Bureau of Refugees, Freedmen, & Abandoned Lands, 1865 - 1870

M810 Records of the Superintendent of Education for the State of Alabama, Bureau of Refugees, Freedmen, & Abandoned Lands, 1865 – 1870

M1900 Records of the Field Offices for the State of Alabama, Bureau of Refugees, Freedmen, & Abandoned Lands, 1865 - 1872

M979 Records of the Assistant Commissioner for the State of Arkansas, Bureau of Refugees, Freedmen, & Abandoned Lands, 1865 - 1869

M980 Records of the Superintendent of Education for the State of Arkansas, Bureau of Refugees, Freedmen, & Abandoned Lands, 1865 - 1872

M1901 Records of the Field Offices for the State of Arkansas, Bureau of Refugees, Freedmen, & Abandoned Lands, 1865 - 1872

M798 Records of the Assistant Commissioner for the State of Georgia, Bureau of Refugees, Freedmen, & Abandoned Lands, 1865 - 1869

M799 Records of the Superintendent of Education for the State of Georgia, Bureau of Refugees, Freedmen, & Abandoned Lands, 1865 1869

M1904 Records of the Field Offices for the State of Kentucky, Bureau of Refugees, Freedmen, & Abandoned Lands, 1865 - 1872

M1026 Records of the Superintendent of Education for the State of Louisiana, Bureau of Refugees, Freedmen, & Abandoned Lands, 1864 - 1869

M1027 Records of the Assistant Commissioner for the State of Louisiana, Bureau of Refugees, Freedmen, & Abandoned Lands, 1865 - 1869

M1905 Records of the Field Offices for the State of

Louisiana, Bureau of Refugees, Freedmen, & Abandoned Lands, 1865 - 1872

M1906 Records of the Field Offices in the States of Maryland & Delaware, Bureau of Refugees, Freedmen, & Abandoned Lands, 1865 - 1872

M1907 Records of the field offices for the State of Mississippi, Bureau of Refugees, Freedmen, & Abandoned Lands, 1865 - 1872

M1914 Records of the Mississippi Freedmen's Department ("pre-Bureau records"), Office of the Assistant Commissioner, Bureau of Refugees, Freedmen, & Abandoned Lands, 1863 - 1865.

M1908 Records of the Field Offices for the State of Missouri, Bureau of Refugees, Freedmen, & Abandoned Lands, 1865 - 1872

M843 Records of the Assistant Commissioner for the State of North Carolina, Bureau of Refugees, Freedmen, & Abandoned Lands, 1865 - 1870.

M844 Records of the Superintendent of Education for the State of North Carolina, Bureau of Refugees, Freedmen, & Abandoned Lands, 1865 - 1870.

M1910 Records of the Field Offices for the State of South Carolina, Bureau of Refugees, Freedmen, & Abandoned Lands, 1865 1872

M1911 Records of the Field Offices for the State of Tennessee, Bureau of Refugees, Freedmen, & Abandoned Lands, 1865 - 1872.

M821 Records of the Assistant Commissioner for the State of Texas, Bureau of Refugees, Freedmen, Abandoned Lands, 1865 - 1869

M822 Records of the Superintendent of Education for the State of Texas, Bureau of Refugees, Freedmen, & Abandoned Lands, 1865 1870

M1912 Records of the Bureau of Refugees, Freedmen, & Abandoned Lands, Texas, 1865 - 1872.

M2029 Records of the Field Offices of the Freedmen's Branch Office of the Adjutant General, 1872 - 1878. (Disbursement Officers)

RECORDS RELATING TO LAND

M68* Lists of North Carolina Land Grants in Tennessee, 1778 - 1791

M145 Abstracts of Oregon Donation Land Claims, 1852 - 1903

M203* Abstracts of Washington Donation Land Claims, 1855 - 1902

M815 Oregon & Washington Donation Land Files, 1851 - 1903

T1008* Register of Army Land Warrants Issued Under the Act of 1788 for Service in the Revolutionary War: Military District of Ohio

M1115 Land Claim Case Files of the U.S. District Court for the Eastern District of Louisiana, 1844 - 1880.

M1382 Bound Records of the General Land Office Relating to Private Land Claims in Louisiana, 1767 - 1892.

M1385 Unbound Records of the General Land Office Relating to Private Land Claims in Louisiana, 1805 - 1896.

T910 California Private Land Claims Dockets 1851 - 1856. (some rolls)

7RA176* Record of Proceedings (Minutes), 1893 - 1895, Alva, OK, Board of Townsite Trustees

7RA177* Alva, OK, Townsite Records: Record of Filings, 18931894; Homestead Contest Docket, 1893-1899; Disbursing Agent's Accounts, 1894-1895; Assessment Ledger, 1893 - 1895; Record of Contest Fees, 1894

7RA200 Townsite records for Blackburn, Choctaw City, Cleo, Edmund, Enid, Frisco, Guthrie, Hennessey, Jonesville, Kingfisher, Newkirk, Oklahoma City, Pawnee, Perkins, Mulhall, Perry, Reno City, Round Pond, Stillwater, & Woodward, Oklahoma

7RA285 Enid, OK: Press Copies & Agent Accounts; Woodward, OK; Abstracts of Cash Entries & Disbursing Agents Accounts

P2279 "Spanish Land Grants in New Mexico", Records of Surveyor General of New Mexico (1854-1892) & Court of Private Land Claims (1891- 1908) use Calendar to the Microfilm Edition of the Land Records of New Mexico for roll list

OTHER STATE DEPARTMENT RECORDS

M2025* Registers of Applications for the Release of Impressed Seamen & Related Indexes

T967 Copies of Presidential Pardons & Remissions, 1794-1893

FEDERAL POPULATION CENSUSES

T1224 1830-1930 census enumeration district descriptions

M1283 Cross Index to Selected City Streets & Enumeration districts, 1910 (microfiche)

OTHER CENSUSES

M1871* Non-Population Census Schedules for Alaska, 1929: Agriculture

M1876 Non-Population Census Schedules for Hawaii, 1930:
Agriculture.

M1896 Non-Population Census Schedules for Puerto Rico, 1930: Non- farm Livestock

XC1* Kansas Territorial Census of 1855

XC2* Kansas Territorial Census of 18561858 XC3* Kansas Territorial Census of 1859

XC4 Kansas Territorial Census of 1860

XC5 Kansas State Census of 1865

XC6 Kansas State Census of 1875

T1136 Non-Population Schedules for Louisiana, 1850-1880

T1175 Schedules of the Minnesota Territory Census of 1857

T1138 Non-Population Schedules for Pennsylvania, 1850-1880

XC16* Oklahoma Territorial Census of 1890

I21 Washington Territorial Census, 1857-1889

M1809 Wisconsin Territorial Censuses, 1836, 1838, 1842, 1846, & 1847

M1791 Schedules of a Special Census of Indians, 1880 (regarding living conditions & health)

M2073* Statistics of Congregations of Lutheran Synods, 1890

M2067 1935 Census of Business

M2070* 1935 Census of Business: Schedules of Radio Broadcasting Stations

RECORDS RELATING TO POSTAL EMPLOYEES

M1131 Record of Appointments of Postmasters, Oct. 1789-1832.

M1126 Post Office Department Reports of Site Selection, 1837-1950 (Texas, Colorado, & California only)

M601 Letters Sent by the Postmaster General, 1789-1836

M2075* Record of Appointment of Substitute Clerks in First & Second-class Post Offices, 1899-1905

M2076* Index & Registers of Substitute Mail Carriers in First & Second-class Post Offices, 1885-1903

M2077* Indexes to Rosters of Railway Postal Clerks, ca. 1883-1902

MISCELLANEOUS

T408* Credentials of Delegates from Virginia to the Continental Congress, 1775-1788

M95 Records of the Officer of the Secretary of the Interior Relating to Wagon Roads, 1857-1887

M1373 Registers of Lighthouse Keepers, 1845-1912.
M63 Lighthouse Letters, 1792-1809

M94 Lighthouse Deeds & Contracts, 1790-1853

M217 Attorney Rolls of the Supreme Court, 1790-1951

M408 Index to Appellate Case Files of the Supreme Court, 1792-1909.

7RA115 Index to Appellants & Appellees to the U.S. Court of Appeals, Fifth Circuit, 1891-1960.

M2007 U.S. Court of Claims Docket Cards for Congressional Case Files, ca. 1884-1937.

M874 Journal of Board of Trustees & Minutes of Committees & Inspectors of the Freedman's Savings & Trust Company, 1865-1874.

Made in the USA
Lexington, KY
29 November 2018